JOHNSON COUNTY PUBLIC LIBRARY

J 639.97 M

17804481

Martin, Louise,
Tigers /

3 2938 00255 5491

#17804481

W9-BLZ-800

J 639.97 M
Martin, Louise, 1955—
Tiger

WITHDRAWN

9-5-89

FRANKLIN-JOHNSON COUNTY
PUBLIC LIBRARY
401 South State Street
Franklin, IN   46131-2545

CD

TIGERS

THE WILDLIFE IN DANGER SERIES

Louise Martin

Rourke Enterprises, Inc.
Vero Beach, Florida 32964

FRANKLIN-JOHNSON COUNT
PUBLIC LIBRARY
401 S. State Street
Franklin, IN 46131-2545

© 1988 Rourke Enterprises, Inc.

All rights reserved. No part of this book
may be reproduced or utilized in any form
or by any means, electronic or mechanical
including photocopying, recording or by any
information storage and retrieval system
without permission in writing from the
publisher.

LIBRARY OF CONGRESS
Library of Congress Cataloging-in-Publication Data

Martin, Louise, 1955-
  Tigers / by Louise Martin.

    p. cm. — (Wildlife in danger)
    Includes index.
    Summary: Describes the five remaining species of
tigers, how people threaten their survival, and efforts to
protect the tiger.
    ISBN 0-86592-995-5
    1. Tigers — Juvenile literature.   2. Endangered species
— Juvenile literature.   3. Wildlife conservation — Juvenile
literature.   [1. Tigers.   2. Rare animals.   3. Wildlife
conservation] I. Title. II. Series:
Martin, Louise, 1955-
Wildlife in danger.
QL737.C23M365   1988
639.9'7974428 - dc19   88-10315
                                           CIP
                                           AC

*Title page photo: Tiger (Panthera
tigris)*

TABLE OF CONTENTS

TIGERS

Tigers look like gentle, huge, orange-and-black striped cats, but they are sometimes thought of as "man-eaters." In fact, people have killed many more tigers than tigers have killed people. About a hundred years ago, there were 100,000 tigers in Asia. In 1973 there were just 5,000. Earlier in this century, there were eight **sub-species** of tiger. Three of these are already **extinct**. Only five are left.

Tigers look like gentle, striped cats

WHERE THEY LIVE

Tigers used to live in many parts of Asia. They were found south of a line which runs from southern Russia across India to southeast Asia. Most tigers now live in India, where there are over 4,000. About 3,000 of these live in the wild. Tigers can live in grasslands, swamps, and forest areas. They need a good supply of water and smaller animals on which they can **prey**. The tiger's favorite food is wild pig.

Tigers need a good supply of water

THREATS TO TIGERS

Human beings are the greatest threat to the tiger's survival. As the number of humans increases, more land is needed to grow food. Whole forests are cut down to provide man with wood for fires, buildings, and paper. Tigers are left with fewer and fewer places to live. The situation in India is a good example. There are now five times as many people in India as there were in 1900. Much of the tigers' land has been taken over by farmers, who also often kill the tigers so they don't eat their animals. The tigers have been pushed deeper into the forests.

Fierce-looking tigers like this frighten farmers

HUNTING TIGERS

Hunting tigers used to be a very popular sport in India. Their beautiful striped skins were used as rugs or hung on walls. The Indian **maharajas** and the **colonial British**, who lived in India, often organized tiger hunts. They would go out into the country for three weeks at a time, just to kill tigers. Sometimes fifty tigers were killed in a single three-week hunt. No wonder 95,000 tigers disappeared between 1900 and 1970!

Tigers like to swim

The Indian tiger population is growing

A pair of Chinese tigers in Shanghai Zoo

"PROJECT TIGER"

In 1973, some people realized there were only 5,000 tigers left in the world. The **World Wildlife Fund**, an organization that sets up plans to protect rare animals and plants, took action. With the help of the Indian government, they launched "Project Tiger". Nine of India's nature reserves were involved in this plan to save the Indian tigers from farmers and from **poachers**, who hunt animals illegally. At the beginning of "Project Tiger", only 300 tigers existed on the reserves. Fifteen years later, there are now 1,200, or four times as many.

An Indian tigress relaxes with her cub

CHINESE TIGERS

Chinese tigers *(Panthera tigris amoyensis)* are on the brink of extinction. These tigers used to roam freely across southern China. Even in 1949, China had as many as 4,000 Chinese tigers. Today, only about fifty wild tigers are left in China. As in India, China's human population has created farmland out of the tigers' land. For years, farmers were afraid of the tigers. They thought the tigers would eat their animals — and maybe them as well. The Chinese government encouraged farmers to shoot tigers because of the danger to both people and crops.

Tigers need vegetation for camouflage

CHINESE TIGERS AND MEDICINE

China's tiger population began to disappear, and the Chinese government looked at the situation again. In 1977, they passed a law forbidding the killing of tigers. As many tigers as possible were put into nature reserves. But some Chinese doctors use tigers' internal organs and bones in their traditional medicine.The bones are made into a wine that people believe cures rheumatism. Because Chinese people are willing to pay a high price for their medicine, poachers still kill tigers, even on the reserves.

A Sumatran tiger rests in the jungle

SIBERIAN TIGERS

The Chinese government is also concerned about another kind of tiger, one that lives in northeast China. The Siberian tiger *(Panthera tigris altaica)* was first endangered in 1870 when the Qing Dynasty, the rulers of China, allowed the forest to be cleared. Scientists think there are only fifty Siberian tigers left in China today. However, about three hundred wild Siberian tigers live in Russia near the Chinese border. There are also six hundred more Siberian tigers in zoos around the world.

A tiger with his prey

HOW WE CAN HELP

The world's tiger population has probably doubled in the past fifteen years, since scientists began to take action to save tigers. We have lost three of our sub-species — the Balinese, the Caspian, and the Javanese — and the remaining sub-species are not safe yet. The third Indonesian tiger, the Sumatran, is rare but still in existence. Governments are helping to set up areas where all the remaining tigers can live undisturbed, where they will not hurt farmer's crops and livestock, and where poachers cannot hurt them.

Glossary

colonial British (cuh LO nee al BRIT ish) - British citizens who moved to other countries governed by Great Britain, such as Kenya

extinction (ex TINK shun) - the end of a species

maharaja (ma ha RA zhah) - Indian prince or king

poachers (POE churz) - people who hunt animals without permission

prey (PRAY) - to hunt for food

sub-species (SUB SPEE seez) - a scientific term meaning a group within a species

World Wildlife Fund - an organization that helps save rare plants and animals

INDEX